BRITAIN'S 🏰 HERITAGE

Family Cars of the 1960s

James Taylor

First published 2018

Amberley Publishing
The Hill, Stroud
Gloucestershire, GL5 4EP

www.amberley-books.com

Copyright © James Taylor, 2018

The right of James Taylor to be identified as
the Author of this work has been asserted in
accordance with the Copyrights, Designs and
Patents Act 1988.

ISBN 978 1 4456 8322 5 (paperback)
ISBN 978 1 4456 8323 2 (ebook)

British Library Cataloguing in Publication Data.
A catalogue record for this book is available from
the British Library.

Printed in the UK.

Contents

1
Introduction: Signs of the Times

When Prime Minister Harold Macmillan famously told the British people that 'most of our people have never had it so good,' he was not talking about the cars they were driving. But he might well have been. For within two years of that famous 1957 statement, the first of a series of really significant new cars would reach British showrooms and, as the 1960s unrolled, private motoring would become available to the average British family like it never had been before.

Those significant new cars were not the only factors, of course. Without the growing prosperity that Macmillan had been talking about, there would have been far fewer customers who could afford them. But just as important was the fact that Britain was entering the motorway era. Britain's first motorway, the Preston By-Pass, had opened in 1958, and the first stretch of the M1 was opened in 1959. So it would become easier to travel by car during the 1960s as the motorway network gradually spread, and long journeys would gradually cease to be a dreadful grind through choked-up towns and cities behind slow-moving lorries.

Even so, it would be several years before motorways reached many parts of Britain. The Bank Holiday traffic jams that had so often made the front pages of the newspapers during the 1950s as families headed en masse for the major seaside resorts were not yet a thing of the past. As more cars were put on the road, the problem worsened before it got better.

The Mini seemed to be everywhere in the 1960s, and its makers wasted no opportunity to point out how modern and sensible it was. 'Why buy a period-piece when you can have a Mini?' reads this advertisement. Why indeed? (Author's Collection)

Minis are made for the times you drive in. Now. Today. First of a new generation of BMC cars brilliantly engineered * to meet the needs of the modern motorist, Minis are easier to drive and handle. Easier to manoeuvre. Easier to park. Easier to service. Easier to afford. Minis *enjoy* their motoring. And so do over a million Mini-motorists who agree: why buy a period-piece when you can have a Mini?

* FRONT-WHEEL POWER: TRANSVERSE ENGINE: HYDROLASTIC * SUSPENSION **AUSTIN MORRIS MINIS**

Prices from £469.15.10 inc. tax. Backed by 12 months' Warranty and BMC Service – Express. Expert. Everywhere.

Self-service petrol stations became widespread during the 1960s. In this 1965 picture, the schoolboy is filling Dad's Vauxhall for him. (Getty Images)

Bizarrely, perhaps, there was not much traffic on the motorways in the beginning, although things had changed by the end of the decade. In the early 1960s, the police quite commonly allowed motor manufacturers to use the motorways for speed testing in the early hours of the morning. Rover, for example, did their level best to get 150 mph out of a new prototype car on the M1 in 1962, coming away somewhat despondently with just 149 mph after repeated attempts.

It could not last. A series of high-speed accidents in fog during November 1965

Parking meters had first appeared in Britain in 1958, and were becoming more and more widespread during the 1960s as city congestion increased. (Getty Images)

persuaded the Government to introduce a 'temporary' 70 mph national speed limit in December 1965, which was made permanent in 1967 by Transport Minister Barbara Castle. Road safety was already becoming a major legislative preoccupation. In 1965, legislation required all new cars to be fitted with anchorage points for seat belts (which were already present on some more expensive cars) – although wearing them did not become compulsory until 1983, and then only for front seat occupants. In 1966, the Road Safety Bill tackled drunk-driving, setting a limit of 80 mg of alcohol per 100cc of blood, and in 1967 the breathalyser was introduced to enable police officers to carry out on-the-spot testing.

Change

If motoring became more accessible to the average family during the 1960s, it also came with new responsibilities. There were some dreadful old cars still on the roads in 1960, and the author vividly remembers an old black Morris 8 which had no floor on the passenger's side in the front and yet was everyday transport for a school caretaker and his family. It was in 1960 that the Minister of Transport, Ernest Marples, introduced the MoT (Ministry of Transport) test, using powers under the 1956 Road Traffic Act. The test initially required a basic check of brakes, lights and steering on any vehicle that was ten years old, followed by a similar check every year thereafter. It is a measure of the horrors that this 'ten-year test' revealed that the qualifying age was reduced to just seven years at the end of 1961.

Meanwhile, society was changing more rapidly than anyone could remember, and inevitably these changes had their effect on the families who wanted a car of their own. There was a Conservative government in power as the decade opened, riding a wave of optimism and growth but soon obliged (in 1961) to impose an unpopular wage freeze as inflation threatened to take a hold. Meanwhile, overall prosperity continued to rise, and younger people in particular began to chafe against the attitudes and assumptions of their elders. There was a distinct sense that

BMC make the cars that make sense.

Frontwheel drive roadholding, Hydrolastic smoothness, space-making transverse engine, strict fuel economy, good re-sale value, widest choice of models – it makes sense to buy BMC.

Major British car maker BMC was a leader in the (relatively) new technology of front-wheel drive on family cars. Sadly, behind the scenes the finances were not adding up. (Author's Collection)

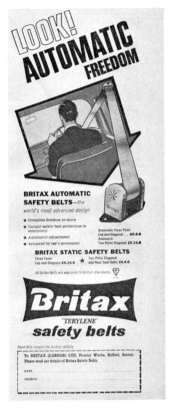

Above left: Safety belts were a novelty in the early 1960s. New cars in the UK had to have built-in anchorage points from 1965, and from 1968 the law required all post-1965 cars to have three-point belts for the front outboard seats. (Author's Collection)

Above right: By the end of the decade, the manufacturing landscape was changing. Most importantly, British Leyland had been created during 1968, bringing together many of Britain's major domestically owned car makers. (Author's Collection)

something new was in the air – and this sense of newness was reflected in the cars introduced as the decade wore on.

Old attitudes certainly were breaking down. In 1960, publisher Penguin Books famously won the right to publish the full D. H. Lawrence novel *Lady Chatterley's Lover*, formerly considered obscene. In 1963, Harold Macmillan resigned as Prime Minister after the Profumo affair, in which his Secretary of State for War was caught up in a scandal involving both adulterous sex and the risk of espionage: it was becoming clear that the prim old guard was not as morally blameless as it liked to believe.

Then, from 1964, a Labour government came to power under Harold Wilson, and for the rest of the decade famously focussed on progress in industry. That kept the idea of progress in the forefront of the public imagination, and the car makers did their best to live up to expectations. But in reality, these were unsettled times, and the old guard was certainly not a spent force. Some old car designs, frankly outmoded by the end of the decade, remained available because there was still a demand for them.

Did you know?

British Leyland

At the start of the 1960s, Austin, Morris, MG, Riley and Wolseley all belonged to BMC (the British Motor Corporation), which had been established in 1952. Hillman, Humber, Singer and Sunbeam belonged to the Rootes Group, which had been founded in 1927. Standard and Triumph belonged to the Leyland Motor Corporation, a bus and truck manufacturer.

Jaguar remained independent, and from 1962 also owned Daimler. Rover, too, was independent, and from 1965 owned Alvis. There were other small specialist car makers, such as Morgan and Lotus, who did not produce family models. When Jaguar and Daimler joined BMC in 1966, the group was re-named BMH (British Motor Holdings).

The Labour government's Industrial Reorganisation Committee, which was run by Tony Benn, had been established to create a more efficient British industrial base through mergers and re-organisation. Benn was concerned that Britain had no motor industry group big enough and strong enough to counter the major groups in Europe, particularly Volkswagen. So he brokered a merger between BMH and the Leyland group, and the result was the formation of the British Leyland Motor Corporation in January 1968. For the time being, few obvious changes were made, although the Riley and Wolseley marques were dropped in 1969.

The Rover 2000 was perceived as an ultra-modern car on its 1963 introduction, and indeed its looks and engineering earned widespread respect during the 1960s. This 1966 advertisement emphasises its safety features – and safety was another new preoccupation in this decade.
(Author's Collection)

AUTOCAR, 23 September 1966

SAFETY IS HOW YOU FEEL <u>NOW</u> IN THE ABSOLUTE CAR

What we mean by Absolute	**The Rover 2000 was designed from the ground up. Planned, from tyres to top, to be the absolute car for its price. Whatever you want from a 2 litre car—you get from the Rover 2000. And then some.**
The Inside Story	The Rover 2000 incorporates more safety features than any other 2 litre car. From the radial ply tyres and disc brakes (four) to the padded parcel shelves and the angled and jointed steering column, safety is what the Rover 2000 is all about.
Confirmation	The Rover 2000 has won the Automobile Association Gold Medal for "the high degree of inherent safety incorporated in the design and construction". This premier award was made for the most valuable contribution to motoring in Great Britain during the year. The most successful 2 litre car in Britain.

ROVER 2000

Price £1,357.9.10 inc. PT.
The Rover Company Limited, Solihull, Warwickshire
London Office: Devonshire House, Piccadilly

Second Class Postage Paid at New York, N.Y.

Choices

Most people who were looking for a family car in the 1960s bought British. This was partly because British makers had larger sales networks than foreign makers and so were easier to find, but there was undoubtedly an element of patriotism in there as well. The big European makers were always represented at the London Motor Show in the autumn, and indeed there were sometimes displays from American and even Russian car makers as well, but foreign cars tended to attract those who wanted to make a statement by being different. They were not mainstream family fare, even though the Volkswagen Beetle certainly did have many adherents. The fact that both Ford and Vauxhall were actually American-owned companies seemed to be conveniently forgotten.

Britain generally tended to look inward, and was still having difficulty accepting that its Empire was in terminal decline and its role in the modern world would have to be different. So probably only a small proportion of family car buyers really cared about whether Britain joined the European Economic Community or not. Harold Macmillan was keen that it should, as he saw an alliance with Europe as the way forward, but Britain's application to join the EEC was vetoed by the French President, Charles de Gaulle, in January 1963. One result was that British cars remained subject to import tariffs in Europe that made them uncompetitive with domestic products. This in turn restricted the number that could be sold, which in turn restricted the expansion of the whole industry during the 1960s. During that decade, French car production increased by 109 per cent, West German production by 94 per cent, Italian production by 189 per cent – and British production by a miserable 21 per cent.

Car makers in the 1960s generally offered a much less varied selection of types than has been common in recent years, and the models on offer were quite rigidly stratified by such factors as price and engine size. Arguably, this reflected the British class system, and arguably it had started to break down in the same way, but this stratification was nevertheless very visible in the models on offer during the 1960s.

For YOUR New Car
INSIST ON
HILLS
THE 'PERFECT FIGURE' NUMBER PLATES

From Your Car Dealer or :—
HILLS (PATENTS) LTD · BOSTON PLACE · LONDON NW1 ... PAD 6601-6

Sex sells... It was quite common for advertising to feature a scantily dressed, pretty girl to draw attention to an otherwise mundane product. (Author's Collection)

Buyers who needed a family car would typically start with something second-hand that might have been built in the 1950s, but for those in a position to buy new, there were some interesting choices. Right at the bottom of the price range were economy cars with engines of 1,000cc capacity or less. The BMC Mini was the standout model, but it was not really typical of the variety on offer. Small and undeniably practical, but not so good for families with growing children, these cars were a step up from the motorcycle and sidecar that had been the lot of so many young families in the 1950s.

It was the models one rung above these that were the aspirational purchases for young couples, though. By 1962, Ford and BMC were both ready with new models that featured the sharp styling which would come to typify the 1960s, and the Ford Cortina and the Morris 1100, priced within a few pounds of one another, would battle one another for sales until the Ford gradually eased ahead. A little further up the scale, in the 1,500cc class, BMC had its Farina-styled saloons, Hillman had its Super Minx, and Vauxhall had its Victor FB. These were cars that announced to the neighbours that you had arrived, were established, and were a thoroughly respectable family.

For those who made it to the top – bank managers, doctors, and financial men (for few women made it so high in their careers) – there was another rung on the family car ladder. These were physically larger models, usually capable of 100 mph or slightly more, and capable of seating five people in quite spacious comfort. BMC had its Austin Westminster and its Wolseley 6/110 derivative – the latter favoured as a police patrol car. Ford had its Zephyrs and Zodiacs, which gained a strong popular image through their use in the police TV drama *Z Cars*. And above that there were Rovers and Jaguars, status symbols as much as genuine family cars, and to some extent out on their own as representatives of all that was good and traditional about British manufacturing.

Yes, it's another posed picture, but Ford was rather proud of the fact that its Anglia was quite widely adopted as a police patrol car – a 'Panda' car, in this unforgettable livery. (Ford UK)

Characteristics

Those who were there at the time will probably remember the interior characteristics of these cars with fondness, although they would baulk at buying a car with similar features today. Most cars had plenty of exposed metal on the dashboard and around the door trims, and that metal was painted the same colour as the exterior panels. Only the more expensive cars boasted wooden dashboards and door cappings. Seats were almost invariably upholstered in vinyl, which could be slippery and even sticky in hot weather, and usually had its own distinctive smell. Leather was found only in expensive models.

Many cars still had rubber floor mats, although carpets were becoming more common; and where a headlining was fitted it was usually made of vinyl. Sometimes the sun visors were padded and trimmed to match the headlining, but at the start of the decade there were still cars with hard sun visors made of tinted Perspex. Windows were universally wound open by hand (although electric operation had been introduced across the Atlantic), and a heated rear window (or rear window demister as it was often known) was a rarity reserved for expensive models. Doors were locked individually by means of the interior handles, and typically only the driver's door had an external keylock.

Engines were invariably petrol-powered – Britain was very slow to accept diesel, except for taxis – and were quite often noisy and asthmatic.

Electric windows were found only on the most expensive cars, but there were kits available to convert standard manual winders to electric power. (Author's Collection)

There were still some old and inefficient side-valve types around, although many were now overhead-valve designs and the very newest had overhead camshafts as well. It was not uncommon to find that the gearbox had only three forward speeds and was operated by a lever on the steering column, which allowed room for one more passenger on the bench front seat. To take the strain during long motorway journeys, overdrive was becoming popular as an option, but automatic gearboxes were rare except on expensive upper-crust models.

get into the driving seat
—now!

There's no need to save for months or years — with the help of Mercantile Credit companies you can get behind the wheel now and drive away.

Ask your dealer for details of Mercantile Credit hire purchase facilities, or contact your nearest branch office — you will find the address in your local telephone directory.

For a friendly discussion of all hire purchase matters, visit us on

STANDS 47 & 48

 MERCANTILE CREDIT COMPANY LIMITED
Elizabethan House, Great Queen Street, London WC2   Tel : Chancery 1234

UNITED MOTOR FINANCE CORPORATION LIMITED
Stoke Park House, Slough. Tel: Slough 23321
 Member of the Finance Houses Association

'But how shall we pay for it, dear?' A car was a major financial commitment, and finance companies were keen to help, as this 1963 advertisement placed in that year's Motor Show catalogue makes clear. (Author's Collection)

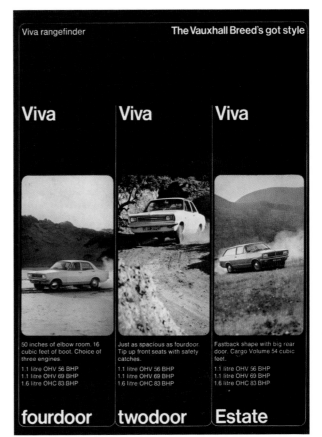

Increasingly, car makers were basing multiple different models on the same design. This 1968 advertisement for the Vauxhall Viva HB model promotes the two-door, four-door and estate versions, each with a choice of three different engines. (Author's Collection)

Did you know?

Purchase Tax

In the 1960s, cars were subject to Purchase Tax in Britain. This was a tax levied on anything considered to be luxury goods, and the money raised went straight to the Government. As cars gradually became seen as a necessity (at least for some people) and not a luxury, there was considerable resentment of this tax.

One result was that manufacturers liked to quote ex-works prices, making the cars look cheaper than they really were. Purchase Tax was often shown separately, leaving the buyer to add the two together and discover the real cost of the car.

As the 1960s opened, the Purchase Tax rate was a massive 55 per cent. It was reduced twice in 1962, initially to 45 per cent in April and then again to 25 per cent in November. This made new cars considerably more affordable, and helped contribute to a vast expansion in car ownership in Britain during the 1960s.

Purchase Tax was finally abolished in 1973, when it was replaced by Value Added Tax (VAT).

Today's top value in family motoring

Take a look and see why. Look at the styling — crisp and clean. Look at the finish — that little bit extra the others haven't got. Then drive it. That smooth, smooth take-off, that effortlessly economical performance. Here's a fine piece of motoring elegance, a superb piece of motoring engineering. A magnificent family car — unbeatable at the price!
See and drive the Hillman Minx '1600' de luxe saloon at your nearest Rootes Dealer.

£634.18.9

£525 plus p.t. £109.18.9

Two-tone colours, overriders, wheel trim discs and whitewall tyres available at extra cost.

■ Low, sleek lines ■ World-proven Hillman '1600' engine for economy and performance ■ Light, positive steering ■ Seating sets high standard of comfort and luxury (front seats have 5" fore and aft adjustment) ■ Front disc brakes for extra safety ■ Suspension designed to give sure, smooth ride ■ No greasing points plus a 3000 miles servicing interval cut maintenance costs ■ Padded facia roll and twin sun visors ■ 4 wide-opening doors ■ Available with the ease and luxury of Borg-Warner fully-automatic transmission as an extra.

HILLMAN MINX DE LUXE SALOON

ROOTES MOTORS LIMITED

Hillman Motor Car Co. Ltd., Division of Rootes Motors Limited
Rootes Ltd., Devonshire House

London Showrooms and Export Division:
Piccadilly, London, W.1.

Above: What could be more British than a cricket match? Nottinghamshire were playing Surrey when this picture of the car park was taken in 1965. Most of the cars visible were new in the 1960s, although there are a couple from the previous decade. (Getty Images)
Left: Not quite so new in concept, perhaps, but new enough to look at, the early 1960s Hillman Minx was seen as a reliable but unexciting family saloon, whatever the advertisement might lead you to believe. (Author's Collection)

2
Starting Out

For a young couple embarking on their new life together, a car came fairly low on the list of priorities. Even when that couple became a family, there were more important things to consider and, if family mobility was an absolute priority, the top choice as the 1960s opened would still have been a motorcycle and sidecar combination. Cars were not yet the universal mode of transport that they have since become, and an awful lot of people still relied on local bus and train services if they needed to go further than a few streets away.

But gradually, and almost by stealth, the car became a family necessity – just as the television had become a family necessity by the end of the 1960s. One reason was that there was full employment by the end of the 1950s (for men, that is; married women were not expected to work even though many did). This was a time of economic prosperity, and young families made the most of it. Relatively speaking, the price of entry into car ownership had come down in the wake of the economy cars that had been popular in the late 1950s, and of course the 1959 Mini had demonstrated vividly that a 'real' car – with four wheels, even if they were very small ones – was now within reach. So, whether they bought second-hand, saved for a new car, or decided to buy one on the 'never-never' (hire purchase was still viewed with suspicion in middle-class Britain), young families were increasingly able to take to the roads.

The temptation was always to find a way of buying new, of course. A new car was likely to be more reliable than an old one, and it certainly carried a social status that an old one

Ford even managed to get some horses into this publicity picture. The car is actually a late 1950s Ford Prefect, but a stripped-out version with a 1,172cc engine became the Ford Popular and was the cheapest new car available in Britain as the 1960s opened. No wonder: the design, called the 100E, dated back to 1953. (Ford UK)

never could. So many young families found a way, somehow, of scraping together the money they needed – between about £500 and about £700 for most of the decade – to get into new-car ownership. That bought a bottom-of-the-range saloon, typically with only two doors. To put its price into perspective, the average house price in 1960 was £2,530, and the average annual salary was about £700. For most of the 1960s, £20 a week was a good living wage.

British car makers were only too ready to cater for that temptation. In the catalogue of the Earls Court Motor Show held in October 1960, the poverty-specification Ford Popular at £515 inclusive of Purchase Tax was the cheapest four-wheel family model to be had. But there was something very right about the Mini, available as either an Austin Seven or a Morris Mini-Minor, for £537; perhaps it was the knowledge that it was British, plus the fact that it was a thoroughly 'modern' car that incorporated a lot of clever design. In between the two at £525 was the evergreen Fiat 500, but there was too much of the economy car about it to attract large numbers of buyers, and there was some (unfounded) mistrust of its rear-engined layout, too. Besides, it was foreign at a time when Britain still believed it built the best cars there were to be had.

Of course, the Mini was rather more than a mere car. During the 1960s it became something of a fashion item as well, and wealthy celebrities like film star Peter Sellers spent large sums on having their Minis customised with wood-and-leather interiors and special paintwork. Ownership of a Mini suggested that our young family was not only fashionable but probably also embraced the progressive thinking of the era – and that mattered in a social context. Above all, though, the Mini was a hoot to drive. It handled like a go-kart (if that was the way you wanted to drive), parked in tiny spaces (increasingly important as cities became more crowded with cars), and had its own cheeky charm because of its tiny size.

The Mini was simply intended as an economy car, but swiftly became an icon. Its transverse engine and front-wheel drive allowed all the space behind to be used for passengers and luggage, and that was why it was so small. This is the very first production car, now belonging to the British Motor Museum collection. (DeFacto/WikiMedia Commons)

THE NEW FORD CONSUL CLASSIC 315   page 33

Good Motoring

ONE SHILLING MONTHLY   JULY 1961

SLEA HEAD page 21

Be a two-car family

Prices from £350 (plus £146.19.2 Purchase Tax) or from £100 down and £13.10.2 per month for 3 years. Twelve Months' Warranty and backed by B.M.C. Service—the most comprehensive in Europe

MORRIS MOTORS LIMITED, COWLEY, OXFORD.
OVERSEAS BUSINESS:
NUFFIELD EXPORTS LIMITED, OXFORD,
AND AT 41-46, PICCADILLY, LONDON, W.1.

We're <u>both</u> going to have a

"QUALITY FIRST"

MORRIS MINI-MINOR

The early 1960s saw the rise of the second car, as Mum increasingly had her own – and a Mini was ideal for the job. This early advertisement has the original and full version of the name, calling the car a Morris Mini-Minor. (MCP)

The Mini's transverse engine was new technology – and yet it was basically a tried and trusted design adapted for the job. DIY maintenance was fully feasible for owners who were so inclined. (Author)

British fashion model Twiggy was a devotee of the Mini, and was among the celebrities who went to specialists Wood & Pickett to have their Minis customised with luxury features. She passed her driving test in this one. (Getty Images)

Ford managed to keep the cost of its entry-level models down, and in 1962 a Ford Anglia two-door saloon cost not much more than a Mini. It was a considerably larger car, too, with pretensions to style and modernity in its reverse-rake rear window. Most buyers probably saw this as a gimmick, although the idea was that the window would remain clean of raindrops in bad weather and would not reflect the sun when the weather was that way inclined. The Anglia sold well, although in truth it was very basic transport for a young family.

There was reasonable room in a Morris Minor for those who could afford one. It was an old design, of course, rounded and almost cuddly and dating right back to 1948. With a bigger engine than the entry-level Mini, the Minor 1000 was still something of a

The Morris Minor was an evergreen model that remained on sale until 1971, having first appeared in 1948. There were both two-door and (more expensive) four-door models, as well as a characterful estate car with wooden-framed body. By the 1960s, it was called a Minor 1000, and from 1962 had a 1.1-litre engine. (MCP)

The Hillman Husky was carefully targeted at young couples, combining estate-car versatility with a low purchase price. Performance was not its strong suit, though. (Author's Collection; Rootes press release)

bargain: £653 as a four-door De Luxe model in 1962, when a Mini cost £515 (Purchase Tax had been cut) and only £709 in 1969 as long as the two-door De Luxe model was good enough. The Minor had something of its own legend, too. In 1961, it had been the first British car to reach a production figure of one million, and its makers had celebrated the fact with a special edition Minor Million in unmistakeable lilac paint. Then there was the fantastically practical Morris Minor Traveller, with a wooden-framed estate body that would take the family dog as well as the growing family and all its luggage. This was another enduring favourite.

Estate cars were catching on fast. Hillman had spotted their value to the young family during the 1950s, and had drawn up the Husky – which was a clever combination of four seats and a van-like body with windows on a shortened Hillman Minx saloon platform. A side-opening tail door and folding rear seats gave maximum practicality, but the Husky was no thing of beauty and was really quite austere. If its 1.5-litre engine was bigger than the norm for this class, it was detuned to give the performance of a smaller-capacity type. The Hillman Husky cost £654 in October 1962 – much the same as a Minor saloon and rather more versatile.

But it was not long after the turn of the decade that the major car makers made a determined assault on the earnings of those young families with some new and devastatingly attractive models. For just a little more outlay – and, surely, it was worth it – from autumn 1962 the

Above: New kid on the block; the 1962 Ford Consul Cortina was a thoroughly modern motor car, even if it was pitched initially at the bottom of the price range. The sharp lines suited early 1960s tastes very well, and the two-door car – like this one – was surprisingly affordable. (Ford UK)
Below: This interior picture of an early Consul Cortina shows the token padding on the hard metal dashboard, the door trims that still left painted metal door tops, and the long, wand-like gear lever. Those seats were upholstered in leatherette – better known as vinyl. (Ford UK)

young family could choose between the brand-new Ford Cortina (strictly called a Consul Cortina at first) and the technically exciting Morris 1100.

The thing about these two was that they seemed to represent exactly what the young family needed. They were more spacious than any Mini, Minor or Husky, they had bigger and more powerful engines that promised top speeds of nearly 80 mph, and they were stylish. The Cortina was clean-cut with a 'big car' look about it, and before long the entry-level models would be followed by high-performance versions that attracted attention on the race tracks as well. It was also devastatingly simple in its mechanical elements. The Morris 1100 had been sharply styled with the assistance of fashionable Italian design house Pininfarina, and it embodied a sophisticated Hydrolastic suspension system (with pressurised fluid as the springing medium), plus the relative novelty of front-wheel drive that gave excellent handling.

In 1962 the four-door Cortina cost £687 in De Luxe form, and the 1100 De Luxe four-door cost £695. Prices would keep pace with one another as these two mass-market family saloons fought for customers, the Ford gradually acquiring sales ascendancy as it was replaced by a visually very different Mk II type in 1966, and also thanks to its wider range of engine options. 'New Cortina is more Cortina' was the advertising slogan, and the public fell for it, making the Mk II Britain's most popular new car during 1967.

This was the rival to the original Cortina – the Morris 1100. The sharp lines were again very much of their times, and had been designed with help from the Italian design house of Pininfarina. Technically, the car was far in advance of the Cortina, with front-wheel drive and a fluid-based suspension. (Author's Collection)

Above: The dashboard of the Morris 1100 was unexciting, although the car was very easy to drive. (Author's Collection)
Below: This sales brochure for the early Morris 1100 – there would be versions with Austin, MG, Riley and Wolseley badges as well – pictures the happy young couple who have settled for one of these advanced cars with its 'float-on-fluid' suspension. (Author's Collection)

By the middle of the 1960s, sharp lines were giving way to more rounded styling. This was the Cortina Mk II, which replaced the original model in 1966. It was gradually moving into a more expensive price bracket, but there was still a two-door model at the bottom of the range – though this is the more expensive GT version. (Ford UK)

Did you know?

Driving schools in Britain during the 1960s tended to choose cars with engines of around 1.1 to 1.3 litres, although there were some that also used smaller cars such as the Mini or the Hillman Imp. The main reason for this choice was probably that these cars were big enough not to give an unrepresentative driving experience. Some were equipped with dual controls, too.

From 1963 there was another important newcomer in the showrooms, as Hillman determined to claim a slice of the Mini's sales with their new Imp. It was introduced at a bargain price of £428 (although the more realistic De Luxe model cost about £25 more) while BMC were busily adding equipment to the Mini and promoting the Super De Luxe version at £493. It was also a completely new venture for Hillman, built in an all-new factory at Linwood, near Glasgow, that eventually became a major headache for the parent Rootes Group.

The Imp offered a different kind of solution to small car design, with a space-saving layout that placed its tiny 875cc engine at the rear, driving the rear wheels, leaving room for a surprisingly large 'boot' in the nose. Unfortunately, some of its advanced features proved troublesome, and word quickly got around. So sales fell short of its maker's expectations and even a series of revisions in the mid-1960s plus some sporty Sunbeam and better-equipped Singer derivatives could not improve the position. Yet many people remember the Imp with fondness, for its cheeky looks, its surprising amount of interior room, and a fun quotient that was higher than its reputation suggested.

Hillman's challenger for the Mini was the Imp, with its engine in the back and a distinctive, sharp-edged shape. This is a 1965 publicity picture, so the car has been dressed up with whitewall tyres that were not a standard feature. The lady seems quite impressed. (Author's Collection; Rootes press release)

A long-term favourite was the Triumph Herald. The Triumph name suggested sports cars and sporting saloons, which tended to give the Herald a certain amount of cachet. The truth was, though, that the Triumph name had been cleverly used on a replacement for the small family Standards of the 1950s. Standard and Triumph were part of the same company, and in the new modern era of the 1960s nobody wanted anything that was simply 'standard'.

The Herald started out with a 948cc engine in 1959, going up to 1,147cc in 1961 for the '1200' model. It was quite old-fashioned in construction, with a separate chassis and body. But its

Triumph turned its Herald into a model for the next class up by fitting a 1.6-litre engine – a six-cylinder, no less. Twin headlamps and the new name of Vitesse did the rest. (MCP)

Look Dad. Fourdoor.

New family-tuned Viva.

Look Dad! Success-story Viva now comes fourdoor too.
For fourdoor freedom. And getting-in-and-out-ease.
1159cc economy or 1600cc power. Deep body-contoured seats.
Fitted front seatbelts. And a 16 cu.ft boot.
Viva fourdoor or twodoor. Now with a safety package
including energy absorbing steering column.
Twodoor from £658. Fourdoor from £759.
Purchase tax paid.

The Vauxhall Breed's got style.

Vauxhall did much the same thing with its HB Viva. From October 1968, what had started out as a two-door saloon with a 1.2-litre engine became available as a four-door with a 1.6-litre engine. (Author's Collection)

chiselled, Italianate looks made it stand out at a time when all things Italian were fashionable in Britain. It genuinely was Italian in origin, too, because Triumph had engaged Italian stylist Giovanni Michelotti to design it for them. At £702 in 1960, dropping to £660 as a 1200 model in 1962, and then to £671 by 1968, it did stretch the new family's budget a bit, but seemed to offer ample rewards. Triumph also offered stylish coupé and convertible derivatives as well, and later on an estate too, but these were all too expensive for family car buyers starting out. The Herald became a driving-school favourite, not least because of its famously small turning circle.

Another driving-school favourite was the Vauxhall Viva, especially in its second iteration as the HB model from 1966. There were several Viva models, including a GT and an estate, and engines went up to 1.6 litres – but the driving school cars were usually base-model two-doors with the 1,159cc engine. They had remarkably light steering and not a lot of performance, which made them ideal for the job. A spacious interior endeared them to private buyers, too.

Then, of course, there was the Ford Escort, which replaced the Anglia in Ford's model line-up from 1968. Like the Viva, the Escort range was extended upwards into a higher price bracket, but the entry-level two-door saloons with just 1,098cc under the bonnet were quite good enough for the driving school. They were actually quite spritely, too, and boasted direct-feeling rack-and-pinion steering, which helped the more expensive 'performance' versions earn a good reputation. Most important, though, was that they offered a good amount of space and were well priced at just under £700 in 1968. This was, of course, the top end of the sector: a Mini could still be had for just over £560.

... AND WHAT
A LOT OF CAR
YOU GET!

This 1964 publicity for the Vauxhall Viva (the boxy original HA model) focussed on the fact that it offered more interior space than many cars in its class. (Author's Collection)

From autumn 1968, the Escort became Ford's entry-level model. There would be more expensive variants later, and the car would have a distinguished competition career as well. But 1.1-litre two-doors like this one were a real aspiration for young couples at the end of the 1960s. (Ford UK)

Did you know?

There was still a lot of American influence on British cars in the 1960s. Paired headlights originated in the USA, and so did the vogue for two-tone paint schemes – although this was dying out before the mid-1960s.

Both Ford and Vauxhall were American-owned, and so it was no surprise that their products should reveal US influences. A notable one was the reverse-rake rear window that Ford used on their Anglia, the 105E model introduced in 1959. The theory behind this was that it would remain clear in the rain. The Anglia was always a two-door saloon (although there were estate derivatives as well), and had engines of just under 1 litre or just under 1.2 litres. The Anglia would give way to the Escort in the later 1960s.

3
Respectable Citizens

For many Britons in the 1960s, respectability and middle age began in their early thirties – although attitudes were changing rapidly and by the end of the decade there were many people who were doing their best to avoid old-fashioned 'respectability' of any kind.

Nevertheless, for the car makers, what mattered was their income and how much of it they were prepared to spend on a new car. So there was a distinct type – even class – of car that was designed to meet the needs of those families who were becoming more established. In broad terms, these cars cost somewhere between £700 and £1,000 inclusive of Purchase Tax, and they had engines with a minimum of 1,500cc, going on up to just under 2,000cc. Road performance was correspondingly better, and when stretched to their limits these cars could typically sweep along the motorways at speeds around 75 mph, and nearer 80 mph by the end of the decade.

If that sounded glamorous at the time, the truth was that most family cars in this sector of the market conformed to a pattern, and this conformity perhaps sat well with a Britain that had not yet shaken off its traditional class structure and values. They had four doors and a conventional 'three-box' design, and several of them had more expensive estate derivatives. Sometimes, these models had smaller-engined and cheaper siblings; the Ford Cortina was typical.

Some of them were old-school models, and that very age gave them a certain respectability. Typical were BMC's 1.5-litre Farina saloons, which had been designed by the Italian styling house in the late 1950s and now came with a variety of equipment levels and badges from humble Morris to plush Wolseley. The Morris Oxford de Luxe saloon cost £872 in October 1962; at the same time, the top model Wolseley 16/60 cost £953. Priced in between them was the practical and roomy Austin A60 Countryman estate version of the range, at £943. It was ideal for family holidays, and ideal for those with dogs, too.

Did you know?

The 'three-box' saloon design, with a projecting boot visually balancing the projecting bonnet, was American in origin. It first appeared on the 1946 Studebakers, and was immediately widely copied. Before that, cars had usually had round or sloping tail panels, and a smaller boot incorporated within those panels.

Ford had the Cortina at the bottom end of this market, always in four-door or estate form to distinguish it from its cheaper siblings. But there was also the highly distinctive Corsair, which had slightly more room than the Cortina and shared a lot of its mechanical elements. Above that came the Zephyr 4 with a four-cylinder engine, and even the Zephyr 6 (with six-cylinder power) came in at just over £900.

ZEPHYR 6 SALOON *feel the thrill of big car power—the pull of 100 horses!*

Above: The Ford Zephyr, in Mk III guise from 1963, gained valuable publicity through the *Z Cars* TV series. It was at the expensive end of its class. The one pictured here shows that the fins popular during the 1950s may have been tamed, but were still very much present. (MCP)
Below: The more expensive variants of the Ford Cortina figured in this class, and none more so than the estate versions. Ideal as family cars, they were also favoured by the Kent Police, who bought this 1965 example. (Kent Police Museum)

In the early 1960s, Ford had still to commit to the Cortina range, and had more than one offering in the 1.5-litre class. This is a 1964 Corsair, its distinctive front-end design making it look less ordinary than it was. (Charles01/WikiMedia Commons)

The Corsair is mainly remembered for two things. One was its sloping, shark-like nose, and the other is the distinctly rough V4 engine fitted from 1966, a 1.7-litre size. The Zephyr, on the other hand, had vestiges of 1950s styling in its fin-like rear wings, but it gained much in the popular imagination from being the police patrol car in the popular TV series *Z Cars*. The Mk III Zephyr, which was the *Z Cars* model, had a more conventional 1.7-litre engine or, as a Zephyr 6, had 2.5 litres, which was way above the class norm. However, the replacement Zephyr Mk IV from 1966 had a 2-litre V4 engine and was a great whale of a car which was doing its best to be credible in the next size up.

Ford's main rival was Vauxhall, and Vauxhall's car in the 1.5-litre class was quite finely judged to give the impression of a larger and more expensive model. The bench front seat and column gearchange standard on the cheaper models helped to give an impression of size and space, and indeed the Victor FB could carry six passengers as long as some of them were children. Although the entry-level price was just over £702 in 1962, the more expensive Super and De Luxe models were more attractive, and the top-of-the-range sporty VX4/90 saloon cost a substantial £927 15s 3d. The '90' in its designation indicated a maximum speed of over 90 mph, and unsurprisingly Vauxhall fitted it with disc front brakes as standard. Its existence had a halo effect on the other models of the range, which were, frankly, rather stodgy machines. There were estate derivatives, too, starting at £812 and going on up to £902 at 1962 prices.

Vauxhall, of course, understood the value of regular product updates, and replaced the Victor FB in 1964 with the more slab-sided Victor FC. Despite a little more power and performance than its predecessor, the FC's less conservative shape was not well received, and Vauxhall quickly responded with a Victor 101 model, its name reflecting the claimed 101 improvements over the superseded FB Victor! There were estate derivatives as well, but the

This was Vauxhall's challenger in the 1.5-litre class during the first part of the 1960s. This 1964 Victor is an FB model, and still has the two-tone paintwork that would soon become unfashionable. (Martin Pettit/WikiMedia Commons)

Victor was by this stage losing sales to the bigger-engined versions of Ford's Cortina. So the Victor FD of 1967 moved up a size, and embraced a 2.0-litre engine as well as a new 1.6-litre type – although the cheapest Victor 2000 still cost well under £1,000. From this point, it was trying to move up a class, perhaps following the example of the big Fords.

Hillman played a very clever game at this level of the market, as they always had. They actually had two models on sale that were mechanically related but had an important price differential. The cheaper car was the Minx; the more expensive one was the Super Minx. The Minx was priced right at the bottom of the 1.5-litre bracket, just within reach of those who might otherwise have had to settle for a rather basic two-door car. This was a proper four-door saloon, with all the additional status that implied, and in 1960 it boasted an engine of nearly 1,500cc with a showroom price of £722. From 1962, that engine size was increased to nearly 1,600cc, and lower Purchase Tax set the price at just £702.

Realistically, the size of the Minx's engine mattered little, because it was an elderly design which gave little more performance than the much smaller engines in the Cortina and BMC 1100. But there was no denying the prestige appeal of 1.6 litres – and from 1962 Hillman made sure that the Series IIIC model carried a '1600' badge quite prominently on each front door to emphasise the fact.

While the Minx deliberately tried to attract both first-time and more mature buyers, the Super Minx was quite specifically aimed at the 1.5-litre class. Introduced in 1962, it had a choice of 1.6 or 1.7-litre engines. Mechanically not all that different from the cheaper and older Minx, it nevertheless did boast disc brakes on the front wheels. The Super Minx was also developed to provide a wider range of models, and there were both estate and convertible

These three Vauxhalls have changed people's ideas

VAUXHALL
VICTOR
£702·5·3 Victor Super £736.12.9.
Victor de Luxe £798.10.3. All-synchro 3 or
4-speed gearbox. 12,000 mile lubrication
interval.

This Victor has changed people's ideas about family saloons. It has set new standards in styling, comfort and easy maintenance. Well over 100,000 people have already chosen it. Join them, and you will find that good design speaks for itself—and for you.

VICTOR
ESTATE
£812·5·3 46½ cu. ft. load space with
rear seat folded. 21½ cu. ft. with 5 adults.
Low axle ratio. Heavy-duty tyres and springs.

The Victor has changed people's attitudes to estate cars, too. Thousands of motorists have bought their first estate car because this Victor version is so unusually elegant and practical. The Victor takes all that room at the back in its stride; it really *likes* being an estate car.

VAUXHALL
VX4/90
£927·15·3 1·5 litres, 4 cyls, 81 b.h.p.
Twin carburetters. Power-assisted brakes
(disc at front). 4 speed all-synchro, floor-
mounted lever.

The VX 4/90 has made motorists think again about 'performance' cars. It has shown that real liveliness and real luxury can go together in a roomy four-door saloon—and still give about 30 mpg. With extra power matched by extra safety the VX 4/90 offers vivid motoring with the velvet touch.

All prices include Purchase Tax

Above: The Vauxhall Victor FB of the early 1960s is seen here in three variants, spanning quite a wide price range. At the top is the family saloon; below are the more expensive estate car and 'performance' VX4/90 models. (MCP)

Below: Hillman's Minx was a 1950s design, but this was the 1961 version, with the newly enlarged 1600 engine. Two-tone colour schemes and whitewall tyres were fashionable in the first half of the 1960s. (Author's Collection/Rootes press picture)

The Hillman Super Minx of 1962 was bigger, newer and more modern looking – and, of course, more expensive. (Author's Collection/Rootes press picture)

versions of the car for those who could afford them; prices in 1962 ranged from £847 for the saloon up to £961. The Super Minxes seemed modern, colourful (Hillman had several two-tone paint schemes) and good value for money in the Hillman tradition. Never lost for ideas, parent company Rootes also developed luxury and sporting derivatives, which they badged as the Humber Sceptre and Singer Vogue respectively, charging appropriately more.

However, Rootes were deeply impressed by the Ford Cortina, and that car had a major influence on the car that replaced both the Minx and Super Minx in 1966. It was called the Hillman Hunter, and it was disappointingly ordinary despite its sharp new shape. Hunters had 1.7-litre engines, in the Hillman tradition of punching slightly above their weight, but they also had 1.5-litre derivatives that retained the Minx name and hovered around the bottom of this class of cars. In 1968, a Hunter cost nearly £970, while the much less well-equipped Minx cost just £830. Sporty Singer Vogue and well-equipped Humber Sceptre variants became available, too, at higher prices.

The 1.5-litre Farinas were really not representative of what BMC could achieve, and in 1964 the company introduced a new model that really should have been a game-changer. Instead, it remained curiously unique. Even so, the Austin or Morris 1800, with plusher and more expensive Wolseley derivatives too, was a quite unforgettable machine. Its use of front-wheel drive and a wheel-at-each-corner layout provided what seemed like a simply enormous passenger cabin, which gave the car a very special appeal.

At £809 for the Austin De Luxe version in autumn 1964, the car was hard to resist as family transport, and that 1.8-litre engine gave it a certain additional cachet as well. What buyers

Above: The sharper styling in vogue by the middle of the 1960s is well illustrated here by a Minx De Luxe. The model was introduced in 1966 but was more common in better-equipped and more expensive form as the Hillman Hunter. (Author's Collection/Rootes press picture)

Right: Ford's Consul Classic 315 lasted only from 1961 to 1963, giving way to the much better-looking Consul Cortina. The front end was modern-looking and quite attractive, but the rear was altogether less happy, and there was nothing very new in the mechanical specification. (MCP)

SET THE STYLE-MAKE THE PACE
WITH THE ALL-NEW CLASSIC

THE ALL-NEW
CONSUL
CLASSIC 315 FROM **FORD** OF BRITAIN

Take a long look at the Classic at your Ford dealer's — book a no obligation test drive as soon as you can.

The BMC 1800, seen here as an Austin, was a brilliant design that should have done far better. As it was, its size and 1.8-litre engine were sometimes perceived as deterrents instead of advantages. (DeFacto/ WikiMedia Commons)

had to live with was idiosyncratic styling (not for nothing was it nicknamed the Land Crab) and a bus-like driving position, but the 1800 could hardly be beaten on value for money. Bizarrely, its makers did not trust it enough to withdraw their older 1.5-litre saloons and give it a clear run in the marketplace.

The real innovation in this area of the market came not from Britain but from France. In 1965, Renault introduced their new 1.5-litre 16 model, which many people would simply have dismissed as being typically quirky in a Gallic way. And so it was, but it offered the versatility of an estate car in a saloon format. The sloping rear of the body was arranged as a tailgate that opened upwards, giving access to the boot and allowing far more loadspace flexibility than in an ordinary saloon. Britons were suspicious at first, but at a price of just under £950, the Renault 16 made sense, and it soon caught on. Renault capitalised by adding better equipped models with larger engines, but the most telling result of the car's arrival in Britain was that British Leyland copied its key features for the Austin Maxi.

The Maxi was intended to replace the old Farina-styled 1.5-litre cars, and it copied the Renault's practical hatchback configuration. Delayed until 1969, by which time BMC had been subsumed into British Leyland, its real impact would come in the next decade – but it did get off to an unpromising start, with poor build quality and a disastrously vague gearchange. It was also strangely proportioned because it used the doors of the Land Crab models to save money. Few people have fond memories of the early Maxi, although later ones were greatly improved.

The 1960s saw the beginnings of serious competition from continental European cars, and the Renault 16 was only the most notable of the models that began to attract respectable British middle-class families. Yet there was another foreign-made car that had been around, seemingly for ever, and still attracted a quite enthusiastic group of buyers. That car was the Volkswagen Beetle.

Over the years, the Beetle has gained the image of a cheap and cheerful low-priced car, but the reality was that import tariffs in Britain initially forced it to compete for sales

Above: The BMC Farinas were great favourites, and not only in Britain. This later example – an Austin A60 – was sold new in Switzerland and is now in enthusiast ownership there. (Author)
Below: BMC had these 1.5-litre saloons styled by the Italian design house of Pinin Farina, and they were always known as the BMC Farinas. This is an early Austin A55 variant, the two-tone scheme being very much of the times and serving to highlight the tail fins that would be toned down on later models. (MCP)

Above: Foreign cars were not yet a serious challenge to domestic products in Britain, but the Renault 16 hatchback from France made car makers sit up and take notice. This is an early 1.5-litre model, a 16 GL from 1967. (Vauxford/WikiMedia Commons)

Below: The Austin Maxi arrived right at the end of the 1960s, and picked up on the versatility pioneered a few years earlier by the Renault 16. Here it is demonstrating what a useful family car it could be. (Magic Car Pics)

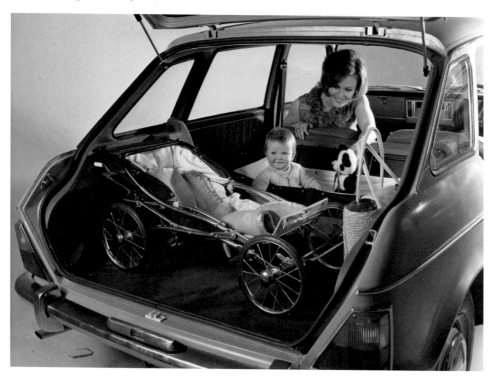

with the lower-priced models in the 1.5-litre class. This was a car with a 1,200cc engine, which by rights should have competed with considerably cheaper domestic products, but it did manage to achieve 72 mph which, its makers claimed, was 'maximum and cruising speed'. It lacked other amenities that buyers often expected at this price, coming with only two doors.

In 1962, the cheapest Beetle cost £717, and in 1964 it was £735. But the importers held their nerve and managed to hold prices down as well. So by 1968 the basic 1200 model cost only £668, while a bigger-engined 1500 De Luxe model with a price of £795 was aimed right at the middle of the 1.5-litre class. By then, distant memories of its origins in Nazi Germany

The car that owes its success to . . .
THE MAN IN THE STREET

THE BEST VALUE IN THE WORLD

VOLKSWAGEN 32-34 ST. JOHN'S WOOD ROAD, LONDON, N.W.8. 'Phone: CUNningham 8000
West End Showrooms: 38-39 Stratton Street, London, W.I. 'Phone: GROsvenor 4666

The VW Beetle ended up punching above its weight, thanks to import taxes, but it gained a strong following. It was indeed 'the car that owes its success to the man in the street' – an interesting twist on the name Volkswagen, which means 'people's car'. (MCP)

Did you know?

The Ford Cortina

Ford's careful development of its best-selling Cortina range began with the Mk II model in 1967. Although there were still 1.3-litre two-door models at cheaper prices, the core of the range was now the 1.6-litre four-door models. Reaching a little higher, from 1968 there was a 1600E variant as well, the E standing for Executive and coming with a more powerful engine, lowered suspension and wood interior trim. Like the Corsair 2000E (see Chapter 4), this was a well-executed attempt to give the mid-range Ford models a flavour of the cars pitched at the growing 'executive car' market.

had receded, and more and more buyers trusted the Beetle. They accepted the need to put luggage into the front end rather than the back, because that was where the engine was mounted, and they put up with the distinctive and relentless thrumming of that engine – which was no less noticeable in the 1500 version than in the 1200. The Beetle was reliable, needed less maintenance than most comparable cars because the engine was air-cooled rather than water-cooled, and was easy to work on if needs be.

4
Making It

The qualities that customers expected in luxury-class saloons during the 1960s were quite straightforward. They wanted a car with presence and with a comfortable and luxuriously appointed interior, which usually meant leather upholstery and real wood for the dashboard and door cappings. They also expected the car to provide good performance with a high top speed and impressive levels of refinement. Luxury saloons were by definition suitable for transporting the family as well because of their size, and many were full six-seaters. A few even ended up being chauffeur-driven; these were cars for those who had 'made it' in life.

Broadly speaking, the luxury class saloon had an engine with a capacity of 3 litres or more. It was considerably more expensive than the large family saloon, too, starting at around £1,220 in 1960 and going on up beyond £2,000, inclusive of Purchase Tax. The main contenders for sales came from Rover, Jaguar, and BMC, with some input from Ford and Vauxhall as well, but the market was already shrinking. Armstrong Siddeley had been a major player during the 1950s but closed its doors in 1960. Although there were certainly foreign luxury models on sale in Britain as well, most were considered expensive and exotic, and none were very common.

Jaguar enjoyed a unique position within the British motor industry, and their saloons combined the wood and leather interiors expected of a high quality saloon with sporting performance. To those of a conservative mindset, there was a faint whiff of disreputability about a Jaguar, not least because they had achieved much the same as Bentley had done many years earlier but at a fraction of the cost. Not that any of this worried Jaguar: they were extraordinarily successful and their main concern during the 1960s was keeping production levels up to meet demand. When they did cut costs, it was by reducing the number of model ranges to just one after 1968, while improving quality.

For most of the 1960s, there were four Jaguar saloon ranges. The lowest priced was the Mk 2 or 'compact' model, with 2.4-litre, 3.4-litre or 3.8-litre six-cylinder engines. If the 2.4-litre car was underpowered for the times, the other two certainly made up for it and even with optional automatic gearboxes were formidable performers. Next up – no bigger inside but with a better rear suspension – were the 3.4-litre and 3.8-litre S-type saloons, and after 1966 these were joined by the 420, which was much the same thing with a different front end and a 4.2-litre engine. Then right at the top came the bloated Mk X, renamed a 420G in 1966, which offered acres of space in a body that wasted quite a lot more in its attempt to appeal to American market expectations. It had the 3.8-litre engine up to 1964 and the 4.2-litre size after that.

There was something quite special about these Jaguars, and the small boy whose father had one was the subject of envy by his classmates. There were enough dashboard instruments and switches to suit a small aircraft and the luxurious interiors had their own distinctive smell. In tandem with a burbling exhaust and vivid acceleration, the effect was utterly seductive. For those who wanted even more of the luxury features, Jaguar offered a pair of Daimler-badged models, one based on the Mk 2 saloon (and featuring Daimler's own 2.5-litre V8 engine) and the other based on the 420 and called the Sovereign.

new grace..new space..new pace

a completely new **JAGUAR**...*a successor*

to the Mark IX, now joins the famous Mark 2 and 'E' Type models

The Jaguar Mark X, although an entirely new car in construction, design and appearance, stems from a long and illustrious line of outstanding models which have been identified during the past decade by the symbols Mark VII, Mark VIII and Mark IX. All have been highly successful in their own right and have formed important links in a chain of development culminating in the creation of the finest car yet to be produced in the Jaguar big saloon tradition—the Jaguar Mark X.

This elegant model is of monocoque construction and is powered by the world-famous Jaguar XK 'S' Type 3.8 litre twin overhead camshaft engine with three carburetters. This highly versatile engine by reason of its flexibility, smoothness and silence is ideally suited for use in such a car as the Mark X where every emphasis has been placed upon refinement of performance. Producing 265 horsepower, the engine, save for minor details, is identical with that fitted to the recently introduced 'E' Type Grand Touring Models, and it endows the Mark X with a degree of performance superior even to the Mark IX which it now supplants. Independent suspension front and rear and disc brakes on all four wheels enable full advantage to be taken of this performance with safety and comfort, whilst the luxurious furnishings and appointments include such refinements as reclining seats, folding tables and high efficiency dual-control heating installation.

With new grace in its smooth flowing lines, with new space in its roomier interior and with new pace in its magnificent road performance, the Jaguar Mark X provides a special kind of motoring which no other car in the world can offer.

 The Mark Ten

O N   S T A N D   1 2 1   E A R L S   C O U R T

London Showrooms : 88 Piccadilly, W.1

Above: Jaguar's Mk X luxury saloon was an enviable family car. It was often accused of being bloated, its size having been gauged to meet US market tastes. The car certainly was big – although not quite as big as artistic licence has made it look in this contemporary advertisement. (MCP)

Below: Jaguar's XJ6 replaced all of the existing Jaguar saloons at the end of the decade, and was highly acclaimed all over the world. It was a comfortable and rapid saloon with excellent handling, and was generally considered one of the best cars available anywhere, at any price. (MCP)

Jaguar had too many different models in production for comfort, and replaced them all with the stunning new XJ6 in 1968. This combined a modern shape that was instantly recognisable as a Jaguar with all the traditional luxury features and a choice of 2.8-litre and 4.2-litre six-cylinder engines to give all the expected performance as well. There were Daimler Sovereign versions from 1969, too. Most competitors wondered how Jaguar did it for the money, and lucky buyers simply revelled in their ownership of a car that was widely seen as the world's best saloon – despite a 1968 price of £2,398 for a 4.2 automatic that was well under a third of what Rolls-Royce asked for their Silver Shadow.

Rovers, meanwhile, were cars for gentlemen – and, at the start of the 1960s, for wealthy maiden aunts as well. The less expensive Rovers then available were the four-cylinder 80 (£1,365) and the six-cylinder 100 (£1,538), the latest derivatives of a line called the P4 range that stretched right back to 1949. Their very age made them conservative, and their upright, dignified (and to some eyes, cuddly) appearance seemed to embody many traditional British qualities. They were utterly dependable, beautifully appointed, but not at all caddish like a Jaguar. Rovers were bought by bank managers and doctors, and although they had a fair turn of performance, their focus was on comfort and appointments. The interior of a Rover P4 was another wondrous place to be for a small boy, with what seemed like acres of high-quality leather and a quite wondrous magic wand of a gearstick.

The four-cylinder 80 gave way to a six-cylinder 95, and the 100 gave way to a 110 with improved performance in 1962, but these were to be the last of the big old Rovers that had earned the affectionate nickname of 'Aunties'. They carried on into 1964, overlapping with

Rovers were not sporting cars, but dignified luxury models. This is a 1964 Rover 110, one of the final examples of the P4 range. They were aimed at the professional classes, and were highly respected in their day. (MCP)

Leather, wood, and a sense of well-being... This was the interior of a Rover 110. The floor-mounted gear lever had a long, cranked handle to leave room for the legs of someone sitting in the centre when a bench front seat like this was fitted. (MCP)

the new Rover 2000 that had been designed as their replacement but ended up taking Rover in a new and very profitable direction after its launch in 1963.

There was a more expensive Rover, too, which in 1960 cost £1,864 with the automatic gearbox option. This was the 3-litre, introduced in 1958 with a six-cylinder engine of that capacity and designed as a more exclusive, lower-volume car. Sleeker and more modern in design than the P4 types, it had all the elegance and presence expected of a Rover, and was designed for comfort rather than outright speed. Performance was enhanced from 1962, and a four-door coupé variant with lower roofline and more rakish look was added, not least to make the cars a more appealing alternative to a similarly priced Jaguar. However, the big transformation came in 1967 when the 3-litre engine was replaced by a much more powerful 3.5-litre V8.

American in origin, this engine had been Roverised for its new job. It added a healthy dose of performance without losing refinement, and gave the top-model Rovers a new lease of life as the 3.5-litre models. They were chosen as transport for government ministers and military top brass, and Her Majesty the Queen later declared that a 3.5-litre Rover was her favourite car – when she had the opportunity to drive herself. Although by most standards these Rovers were outdated by the end of the 1960s, they remained firm favourites.

Jaguar and Rover were both of course small independent manufacturers as the 1960s opened, even though they later became part of the same British Leyland combine. But they were not alone in offering luxury-class saloons, because there were some strong contenders from the mass-market manufacturers as well.

Probably the most credible of these was Humber, the luxury marque of the Rootes Group that owned Hillman and Singer. As the 1960s opened, the company had two models based on

Above: Still traditional in looks, but newer, was the Rover 3-litre or P5 model. 1965 was the last year for two-tone paintwork on these cars. (Author)
Below: This was the luxurious interior of the Rover 3-litre. (Author's Collection)

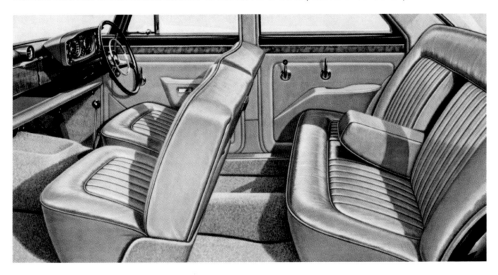

the same bodyshell, the four-cylinder Hawk (from £1,240) and the six-cylinder Super Snipe (from £1,489). Both also had Touring Limousine and Estate derivatives at higher prices. As a contemporary advertisement for the Super Snipe had it, the 'deep leather seats... luxurious carpeting, the walnut trim, occasional tables, the air of discreet elegance... all have been designed to make your every journey an extraordinarily pleasurable experience.'

A direct competitor for the 3-litre Rover was the Humber Super Snipe, again with a 3-litre, six-cylinder engine. (Charles 01/WikiMedia Commons)

The Super Snipe had a restyled roofline from 1964 and from 1966 was joined by a derivative called the Imperial, with power steering and automatic gearbox as standard. This was intended to counter the anticipated threat to sales from the Vanden Plas 4-litre R. But the whole range disappeared in 1967 as new owners Chrysler re-organised the old Rootes Group, and the big Humbers were not replaced.

Mass-market manufacturer BMC also had a foothold in the 3-litre class during the 1960s. Its cars are collectively remembered as the Big Farinas – bigger cousins of the 1.5-litre saloons designed by Pinin Farina – and came with Austin, Wolseley and Vanden Plas badges (in ascending order of cost and plushness). All except one had the same 3-litre, six-cylinder engine, and both automatic and manual-with-overdrive gearboxes could be had. Driving dynamics were not a strong suit, even though the police often favoured the Austin A110 Westminster or Wolseley 6/110 for patrol duties, and maximum speeds were generally only a little over 100 mph.

Keen prices helped these big BMC models gain sales. In 1960, the Austin A99 De Luxe cost £1,219, the Wolseley 6/99 Automatic cost £1,326, and the Vanden Plas Princess 3-litre Automatic cost £1,467. But the cars' real appeal was their beautifully appointed interiors, with leather upholstery and wood trim worthy of much more costly models. Keen to grab more of the market (and to use work done on an aborted joint project with Bentley), BMC introduced the Vanden Plas 4-litre R in 1964, with a cosmetically re-worked 'Big Farina' body and a 175 bhp, six-cylinder Rolls-Royce engine. Unfortunately, its price of just under £2,000 was not matched by its abilities, and the 4-litre R disappeared in 1968 along with the other Big Farinas.

The Austin, at least, was replaced. A new Austin 3-litre was announced in 1967, but its use of the spacious centre section of the BMC 1800 'Land Crab' was too obvious and the car's handling fell below standards expected by this stage. Sales were poor, and the model only just staggered into the 1970s.

One reason why customers were expecting higher standards of handling in luxury cars was that the early 1960s had seen the rise of an entirely new breed of car at the lower end

Above: The Vanden Plas 4-litre R combined a Rolls-Royce engine with an expensively trimmed and modified version of an Austin body, but it failed to attract the anticipated customers. (Author)
Right: This was the car from which the Vanden Plas 4-litre R was derived. It was an Austin Westminster, positioned at the bottom end of the luxury market and, like other BMC products, featuring styling by the Italian Pinin Farina company. (MCP)

A99 Westminster, 6 cylinders, 2.9 litres, Overdrive, Disc brakes.   THE AUSTIN MOTOR COMPANY LIMITED · LONGBRIDGE · BIRMINGHAM

Beyond the glass doors lie warmth and music. Silver gleaming in candlelight, wine glowing like rubies. A world of elegance and sophistication, of laughter and beautiful clothes. And for this kind of evening, this kind of world—the Austin A99.

This is a beautiful car, whose smooth and gracious lines convey an unmistakable

AUSTIN LOOKS YEARS AHEAD

suggestion of purpose and prestige. The great power of the engine—nimble and light in traffic, full throated on the open road—stands ready to serve you. The inherent safety of the car will protect you on your way. This is an Austin, anticipating the future to bring you today's most distinguished motoring, looking—as Austin always does—years ahead.

of the price sector. This was the 'executive' car – smaller, nimbler, more modern in outlook but lacking none of the comfort or luxury associated with traditional luxury models. Rover are generally credited with establishing the type with their 2000 saloon of 1963, although in fairness they had never intended to establish a new class of car but simply to develop a new model that fitted with the requirements and tastes of the times.

What really created the executive car was a combination of increasing prosperity at the start of the 1960s and changes in taxation which favoured company cars at a particular price level. That the Rover led the way was largely due to the prestige associated with the Rover name. When that was combined with an attractive, modern and technically advanced new four-door saloon design, it signalled something new. Business executives whose careers were on the rise could appear forward-looking by embracing the new and the avant-garde while at the same time retaining safe roots in the respectability of the established order.

When the Rover 2000 was introduced in October 1963, it cost just over £1,264, inclusive of Purchase Tax. Price-wise, it was therefore more expensive than a large family saloon, but less expensive than a luxury model. There were a few imported cars at similar prices, but as their showroom costs were generally inflated by import tariffs they were not really competitive with the Rover. The nearest and most obvious domestic competitor was the Jaguar 2.4-litre at £1,348, although Triumph's new 2000 saloon (which cost a lot less at just over £1,094) would soon be seen as a challenger.

The new breed of 'executive car' was typified by the Rover 2000, a thoroughly modern machine with much of the appeal of a traditional luxury saloon in a smaller package. (Author's Collection/Rover press picture)

Above: The Triumph 2000 was slightly cheaper than the Rover but aimed at a similar group of buyers, and it also included an elegant estate version after 1965. (Vauxford/WikiMedia Commons) **Below**: The small Jaguar saloon was never intended as an 'executive car', but it became one by default during the 1960s. This is the final 240 version, with the 2.4-litre engine. (Author's Collection/ Jaguar press picture)

The Rover had its faults, and one of them was a distinct lack of legroom in the rear. Its engine also had only four cylinders, while buyers who spent (or whose companies spent) this sort of money tended to expect the refinement of a six-cylinder. But it became something of a sensation, and its appeal to successful professional people and to middle managers whose careers were on a clear upward trajectory had an undeniable impact on family cars sold in Britain for the rest of the decade.

Other makers scrambled to create cars for the new 'executive' market. Humber positioned their new Sceptre – introduced at the same time as the Rover and initially based on the Hillman Super Minx – as an 'executive' model, although it was both cheaper and less well respected than the Rover. Ford created the Corsair 2000E in 1967 by adding equipment to their existing medium-sized saloon, although its rough and noisy V4 engine did the car no favours. Vauxhall's VX 4/90 had started out as a sporty version of the Victor in 1961, but subsequent versions were given 'executive' appeal to meet the new market demand.

All the first 'executive' models of the 1960s were four-door saloons, although Triumph did well with an estate version of their 2000 from 1965, and even Rover granted factory approval to an aftermarket estate conversion that was built in small numbers from 1968. But the real changes in this market during the later 1960s were improvements in performance. After delivering a twin-carburettor version of the 2000 in 1966 that could reach 107 mph, Rover followed through with a 3.5-litre V8 model (called the 3500) that could touch 114 mph in 1968. Triumph had a 105 mph petrol-injected 2.5-litre car from 1968, although its engine proved troublesome.

Even Vauxhall got in on the act in 1968 by putting their big 3.3-litre six-cylinder engine into the Victor FD to create the 107 mph Ventora – although it was pretty obvious that this was not a pocket luxury saloon in the same mould as the leaders in the executive saloon

Ford tried to break into the 'executive' market with the Corsair 2000E, a better-equipped version of a cheaper model. (Ford UK)

Above: A wooden dashboard was expected in a luxury car – and so the Corsair 2000E had one. (Ford UK)
Below: Ford offered models on the fringes of the top class in the early 1960s, but the reality was that the Mk III Zodiac was a better-equipped Zephyr 6, which belonged to the class below. (Ford UK)

The 1966 Mk IV Zodiac was a large family saloon, with a well-equipped top model called the Executive model for fairly obvious reasons. Unfortunately, its handling left a lot to be desired. (Ford UK)

market. The Ventora was really just a big saloon car with a big engine – priced to reflect its size in much the same way as the big saloons from Ford, the Zephyr and Zodiac. Luxury was not part of the equation (although Ford managed to introduce some tacky fake luxury into their cars), but for those who wanted a big car for its ability to tow a caravan with ease and stability there were few better options.

Did you know?

Special Tyres for a Special Car
Tyre manufacturer Dunlop developed a special low-profile tyre for the Jaguar XJ6, which was used exclusively on the car from its 1968 launch until 1979. The tyre was developed from Dunlop's SP Sport range, and used the same 'aquajet' drainage system. It was classed as an E70VR15 type at the time – a size subsequently better known as 205/70 VR 15.

5
Pushing the Boundaries

The arrival of a family had the same effect on a young man's motoring ambitions in the 1960s as it does today. The dream of a sporty, glamorous, high-performance car had to be sacrificed in favour of the reality of a family saloon that could carry children, push-chairs and other paraphernalia (not to mention the occasional in-law as well).

However, a few manufacturers were offering some hope by the middle of the decade, and none more so than MG. Their recipe was quite simple: take the existing MGB roadster, give it a fixed roof and somewhat token rear seat, and call it a 2+2. It was still a sports car, still an MGB, and had just about enough practicality to serve as everyday transport for a young family for a few years. All that was needed was a sympathetic wife and, quite possibly, a bit of persuasion.

So MG introduced the MGB GT in 1965, getting its fixed-head coupé body drawn up by the Italian styling house of Pininfarina (the name had been presented as a single word since 1961). It was heavier than the MGB roadster, and inevitably not quite as fast, but it was a legitimate sports car with a 104 mph top speed and its price was just under £1,000.

Jaguar followed much the same reasoning, although their E-type 2+2 was aimed at the decidedly wealthy young family with quite a lot more money to spend: on the car's introduction in autumn 1966, it cost nearly £2,285 – and that, frankly, was well into luxury saloon territory.

The MGB was well established as a sports car by the time the GT version was announced. Suddenly, there was a sports car that just might work as a family car too... (MCP)

Above: In truth, there was not a lot of room in the back of an MGB GT, but there was less concern about safety in those days than there is now. (MCP)

Below: How about this for the wealthy young dad? Jaguar's E-type was already the next best thing to a cultural icon when it arrived in 1966. What a pity the 2+2 version demanded some compromises to the otherwise beautiful shape. (MCP)

Not quite as expensive as the E-type 2+2, but certainly a result of the same thinking, was the Lotus Elan +2. The back seat was ideal for kids – because adults could not fit into it. (MCP)

Nor was the 2+2 E-type quite the aesthetic success that the MGB GT undoubtedly was, because lengthening the Jaguar's wheelbase by 9 inches and changing the shape of the fastback body to make enough room for a rear seat had unbalanced the car's proportions.

But it was still a proper Jaguar, even if a compromised one, and that earned it customers. So much so that specialist sports car maker Lotus tried the same trick a year later, announcing the Elan +2 in 1967. It was never going to have mainstream appeal, but an Elan +2 for £1,923 attracted a few fairly well-off die-hards who simply could not face buying an ordinary family saloon just yet.

Unquestionably the biggest success in this field, though, came at the end of the decade, and this was the Ford Capri. Ford had been watching developments closely, and their slick marketing operation understood exactly the dilemma that the young husband faced when having to give up his beloved sports car for a mundane saloon as young couple became young family. So the Ford Capri was advertised as 'the car you always promised yourself', and it cleverly combined the feel of a sports coupé with most of the practicality of a saloon. What's more, it was keenly priced to ensure that it was affordable by its target customers.

Part of the inspiration for the Capri came from the astonishing success of the Ford Mustang in the USA, but this was a very European car that was based on the platform and running-gear of existing European Ford saloons. Introduced at the start of 1969, it was priced at £971 as a 1600, £1,127 as a 2000GT, and £1,291 as a top-model 3000GT. That set its mid-range models roughly on a par with cars like the Austin Maxi (£979), Hillman Hunter (£990), Renault 16 GL (£1,028), or Morris 1800 (£1,078), all of them qualifying as medium-sized family saloons. The far more cramped MGB GT cost £1,269, which makes clear how strong the appeal of the sporty Capri was.

Even so, the Capri had its disadvantages. Most models were not as fast or sporting as their looks suggested. None of them had enough rear legroom once the family started

We were going to call the new Capri a 2+2. But there's too much room in the back.

Above: This was the car that really broke the mould in Britain. The Ford Capri – 'the car you always promised yourself' – could quite easily cut the mustard as either a family saloon or a sports coupé. (MCP)

Left: Subtle this advertisement was not! However, it does show the way Ford tried to sell the Capri as a four-seater and not just a sporty coupé. (Author's Collection)

growing, and the two-door configuration was difficult when dealing with small children. The 2000GT in particular was noisy and was lumbered with Ford's unloved 2-litre V4 engine. However, none of that deterred buyers, and the Capri went on to become one of Ford's greater success stories. What buyers paid for was an image and that, largely, was what they got, even though the 3000GT was also considered to be one of the great performance bargains of its time.

6

What Now? The Old Car Hobby

If reading this book has brought forth the odd wry smile as you remember the family cars of the 1960s, then the business of writing it will have been worthwhile. Those distant memories will be enough for many people, but there will also be many readers of this book who have the inkling of a desire to take their interest further.

Most of the cars of the 1960s have of course now disappeared. It was an era in which the problems of corrosion were poorly understood, and large numbers of 1960s family cars have now simply rotted away into oblivion. Many more were broken up for scrap after their useful lives were over – which typically meant when the likely cost of repairs exceeded the value of the car and the interest of the owner.

However, the more positive news is that, actually, an awful lot of family cars from the 1960s do still survive. One of the key reasons, surely, is that those members of the Baby

Most cars of the 1960s have now ended up like this; all the ones visible here are Triumph models. Scrapyards can sometimes be a useful source of parts, but most 1960s models have been crushed by now. (MCP)

Boomer generation who knew them when they were new are now in many cases middle-aged or older citizens with plenty of time on their hands, plus enough money to indulge themselves in an absorbing hobby. And there can be few hobbies as rewarding as keeping a cherished old car in running order and taking it out for a run whenever the weather and other circumstances permit.

However, there are one or two things to think about before you join the happy band of old-car owners – and there are many thousands of them in Britain, as well as a strong network of specialists able to support owners. Never forget that the family cars of the 1960s have very different characteristics from their modern equivalents. The ones that interest you – their shapes, their smells, their quaintness – are only part of the story. These cars do not drive like modern cars, typically being slower, more cumbersome, and taking longer to stop. Their controls need more concentration, and often more physical effort. They have fewer safety features, and are far less forgiving if the driver makes a mistake.

So if you are not prepared to accept all these differences – if you think of them as primarily shortcomings – you may not find the ownership of a family saloon from the 1960s an enjoyable experience. On the other hand, if you are happy to accept the cars for what they are, can be content if you are not the first away from the traffic lights, and do not expect your car to corner like a go-kart, you will probably discover just how much pleasure there can be in going for a leisurely drive.

Did you know?

Restoration

Many classic car enthusiasts embark on the restoration of the car of their choice, and the amount of skill and effort required for such a task will of course vary between one car and the next. Cars in the 1960s were simpler than their modern equivalents, but many contain some complexities that require specialist help.

A full-scale restoration can take a very long time, and can be very expensive unless you have all the necessary skills yourself. But you don't have to go that far. You may only want to 'recommission' a car that has not been used for some time, and to make sure everything works as it should. Many people find a great deal of satisfaction in the less demanding tasks, whether it is freeing off a seized carburettor linkage or persuading a jammed window winder to work!

The Next Stage

So, if all that sounds like fun, how would you go about finding a 1960s car to enjoy as a hobby? You may of course be extremely lucky and have been left just such a thing by an elderly relative. In that case, your connection to the car will be very direct and very personal, because it does not just represent your memories of the time but actually embodies them as well. But such lucky owners are few and far between.

Finding an old car to enjoy involves both determination and luck. First of all, you need to decide what sort of car it is that you want, and to be honest about how far you are prepared to deviate from the ideal. You also need to be ruthlessly realistic about why you want the car and about how much effort you are prepared to put into its ownership. The pipe-dream of going out for a potter around country lanes on summer Sundays has to be tempered with the reality of the time you will need to spend in keeping the car looking good, the money you may have to spend in fettling and repairing it (or, if you have the necessary skills yourself, the time you will need), the frustration of not being able to find vital spares the moment something breaks, and so on.

On top of that, you will need to spend time and effort on finding the car in the first place. It's as well to forget about those astonishing 'barn finds' that make the news – cars stashed away in garages and barns many years ago that have survived in time-warp condition – because the reality is that there are very few of those and quite often there is intense competition to bid for them when they do turn up. It is much more likely that you will find the car you want by going to a few classic car events and by talking to existing owners. That way, you will also learn a lot about the pitfalls and problems of ownership before you commit yourself irrevocably.

By visiting such events – and there are many of them all over the country between about Easter and roughly the end of September – you may also get a feel for the type of support you might be able to find from the owners' club for the model that interests you. Many of the owners' clubs are first-class organisations that are run by dedicated volunteers, but it is worth remembering that the biggest and most active clubs tend to be for the glamorous cars – typically the sports cars – and not for the family saloons. Even so, there are often overlaps of interest, because the sports models often depended on mechanical elements drawn from the family models.

Club events and summer transport shows are another way of getting to grips with what is out there. This picture was taken at a Mini enthusiasts' event. (MCP)

You might need to get used to autojumbles, where stallholders display all manner of used parts for sale. This picture was taken at a Land Rover event. (Author)

Did you know?

Road Tax, MoT tests and Insurance

For some time now, older classic vehicles have been exempt from road tax in Britain. At the time of writing, any vehicle over forty years old is exempt from road tax and also – somewhat controversially – from the need to be put through an annual roadworthiness test (or 'MoT' – the initials come from the now-defunct Ministry of Transport, which initially established tests for older cars).

However, the onus is still on the owner to maintain the car in a roadworthy condition, and for that reason many classic owners submit their cars for a voluntary check-over once a year. Your local garage can advise you on this.

Many insurance companies offer special policies to cover classic vehicles, and it won't take you long to find one that does so by trawling the internet. Or ask fellow classic vehicle owners; many will have recommendations that you will find useful. Classic insurance is usually very much cheaper than everyday car insurance (unless your classic is worth a great deal of money), and is typically subject to an annual mileage limitation as well. Don't worry: these limitations will give you plenty of leeway to enjoy your cherished classic car!

Discovering More

There are also many magazines to discover that cater for classic car owners, ranging from weekly 'newspapers' such as *Classic Car Weekly* to more expensive and lavish monthly publications like *Classic & Sports Car*. On top of that, it is quite likely that one or more books have been published about your chosen marque, or even about your chosen model, and it is worth making a few enquiries to see what is out there. However, do not assume that a book will be readily available just because it exists: typically, specialist books like these have relatively small print runs, and you may have to spend some time looking for the one about your chosen model, especially if it was published some years ago.

Museums and Archives

Another painless way of getting into the old car hobby – with specific reference to 1960s family saloons, of course – is to take a leisurely wander around some of the major museums where examples of your chosen model and many others are likely to be on display. As examples, try the British Motor Museum at Gaydon (www.britishmotormuseum.co.uk), the National Motor Museum at Beaulieu (www.nationalmotormuseum.org.uk), the Haynes International Motor Museum at Sparkford (www.haynesmotormuseum.com) or the Lakeland Motor Museum at Newby Bridge (www.lakelandmotormuseum.co.uk). There are many more, all over the country, and local tourist information centres will usually be able to direct you towards what is available and can give you information about opening times as well.

Some of these museums also have extensive archives where you can find out more about the car that interests you. For many manufacturers, it is possible to trace individual cars to find out when they were manufactured, which dealership sold them, and often details of

Museums are a good place to get your interest fired up. There's nothing like seeing the real thing instead of pictures. This is one of the halls in the Haynes Museum at Sparkford. (Ian Kirk/WikiMedia Commons)

their original specification as well. All this can be a fascinating adjunct to the business of actually owning and running a family saloon from the 1960s.

Words to the Wise

Finally, here are some words of advice from one who has been involved with old cars for a very long time.

Older cars that remain of interest are generically known as 'classics', a term which implies that there is something special about them. In all honesty, many of the family saloons of the 1960s were not that special – what makes them special today is the fact that they have survived. Sadly, there are plenty of snobs in the old car movement who look down on the ordinary family models that have managed to survive into the present, simply because they were not glamorous, expensive, exclusive or successful in motorsport. Take no notice of them: you know why you are interested in your car, and it is clearly not for the reasons that they are in the hobby.

You may become very attached to the car of your choice, and you may want to embark on a programme of improvements to return it to the condition it would have been in when it left the factory. If so, good luck to you, but do remember that this kind of dedication can become very expensive and very time-consuming, and in all probability will not be shared to the full by other members of your family. Try to keep a sense of proportion at all times; sometimes, it really is more important to visit a distant relative for tea than to attend the annual National Rally of your chosen club. Above all, remember that you became interested in all this because of the fun it offers, and that once it stops being fun, you would be well advised to review why you are doing it at all.

If this picture frightens you, then make sure you have a handy specialist nearby before buying a classic car! The front cover and water pump have been removed for work; the car is a Rover 3.5-litre. (Author)

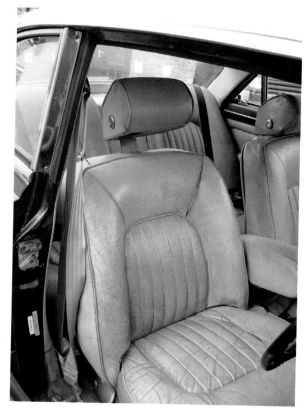

Right: This leather seat is looking tired, but can be made to look like new with a bit of work. (Author)
Below: If you feel able to do major mechanical work yourself, so much the better. This is a Triumph overdrive gearbox that has been removed for work. (Macflip/ WikiMedia Commons)

Did you know?

Collecting Scale Models

Many classic car enthusiasts also collect scale models of the cars that interest them. In some cases, these will be the Dinky Toy, Corgi or other die-cast metal models that were around as toys when they were children, but there is also a sizeable industry that is dedicated to producing accurate scale models of all kinds of cars that interest enthusiasts. There are types to suit all pockets – from a few pounds up to several hundred pounds – and there are several different scales.

The larger scale models are usually the most expensive, and often the most detailed. The problem with these is their size: where do you keep them? Many enthusiasts settle for the 1/43 scale, which is a good compromise; the models are small enough not to present major storage and display problems, and detailed enough to be satisfying to the collector.

Start by visiting an autojumble and seeing what is for sale. Typically, there will be old and damaged toys as well as brand-new scale models for the 'collector' market. For the more exotic models, go online. There is inevitably a challenge of sorts in finding all the available models of your chosen car – and it is certainly cheaper than owning the real thing!

Collecting scale models can be an absorbing adjunct to the hobby, or indeed a hobby in itself. There are some superb examples available, as this collection of British cars of the 1960s makes clear. (Author)